W9-CFL-536

ORANGE COUNTY
HIGH SCHOOL LIBRARY

WILLIAM H. TAFT

SEAL OF THE PRESIDENT OF THE UNITED STATES · E PLURIBUS UNUM

PRESIDENTIAL ✦ LEADERS

WILLIAM H. TAFT

MICHAEL BENSON

ORANGE COUNTY
HIGH SCHOOL LIBRARY

LERNER PUBLICATIONS COMPANY / MINNEAPOLIS

To Mitch, Kim, and Jackson Highfill

The author would like to thank the following, without whose help writing this book would have been impossible: Lisa, Tekla, and Matthew Benson, Anne Darrigan, Jake Elwell, Lee Engfer, Ray Henderson, and the William Howard Taft Historic Site in Cincinnati, Ohio.

Copyright © 2005 by Michael Benson

All rights reserved. International copyright secured. No part of this book may be reproduced or transmitted in any form or by any means—electronic, mechanical, photocopying, recording, or otherwise—without the prior written permission of Lerner Publications Company, except for the inclusion of brief quotations in an acknowledged review.

Lerner Publications Company
A division of Lerner Publishing Group
241 First Avenue North
Minneapolis, MN 55401

Website address: www.lernerbooks.com

Library of Congress Cataloging-in-Publication Data

Benson, Michael.
    William H. Taft / by Michael Benson.
        p.   cm. — (Presidential leaders)
    Summary: A biography of William Howard Taft, the twenty-seventh president of the United States and the only person to serve in both that office and as chief justice of the Supreme Court.
    Includes bibliographical references and index.
    ISBN: 0–8225–0849–4 (lib. bdg. : alk. paper)
    1. Taft, William H. (William Howard), 1857–1930—Juvenile literature. 2. Presidents—United States—Biography—Juvenile literature. 3. Judges—United States—Biography—Juvenile literature. 4. United States. Supreme Court—Biography—Juvenile literature.
    [1. Taft, William H. (William Howard), 1857–1930. 2. Presidents.] I. Title. II. Series.
    E762.B46 2005
    973.91'2'092—dc22   2003022683

Manufactured in the United States of America
1 2 3 4 5 6 – JR – 10 09 08 07 06 05

CONTENTS

———— ✧ ————

President Taft attends a baseball game in Washington, D.C., in 1910.

INTRODUCTION

The game of baseball is a clean, straight game.
—William Howard Taft, 1912

Opening Day of the baseball season on April 14, 1910, was a beautiful spring day. Thousands of fans of the Washington, D.C., team, the Washington Senators, had left work early or skipped school to go to the ballpark. Among those playing hooky was the president of the United States, William Howard Taft, who was sitting behind the dugout at National Park (which was later renamed Griffith Stadium).

During the break before the Senators batted in the bottom half of the seventh inning, President Taft, feeling a little stiff, stood up in front of his seat and began to stretch. Thinking that the president was about to leave, perhaps to attend to some official business, the rest of the crowd stood up to see. And, at six feet two inches tall and weighing three hundred pounds, Taft was easy to see.

The president chuckled, amused by the crowd's reaction. His amusement only increased when, after he sat back down, the crowd returned to their seats as well. This incident started the custom of the seventh-inning stretch. At all professional baseball games, the spectators rise from their seats and stretch and sing for a few minutes before sitting back down to enjoy the rest of the game.

The man who could focus the crowd's attention at a ball game, whose huge smile could be seen from far away, even through his mustache, hardly seemed like the same person who came to be known as the "reluctant president." Taft enjoyed ball games, but he didn't much care for being president. He never wanted the job, and he had not tried very hard to get it. He dreaded each time he had to speak in front of an audience, and he felt he lacked the personality to be a leader. Yet somehow he had risen to the highest office in the land.

CHAPTER ONE

SON OF A JUDGE

Mediocrity will not do for Will.
—Alphonso Taft, William Howard Taft's father, 1869

William Howard Taft was born on September 15, 1857, in Cincinnati, Ohio. Even as a baby, he was big. When William, called Willie or Will by his family, was less than two months old, his mother described him in a letter to a friend: "He is very large [for] his age and grows fat every day."

Will's father, Alphonso Taft, was born in Vermont, the son of a judge. Alphonso moved from New England to Cincinnati in 1838 to start a law practice. His first marriage, to Fanny Phelps, lasted from 1841 until 1852, when Fanny died of tuberculosis. Alphonso and Fanny had two sons, Charles and Peter.

Alphonso met his second wife, Louise, the year after Fanny's death. While vacationing in New England, Alphonso was introduced to Louise at a party held by her father, Boston merchant Samuel Davenport Torry, at their home in Millbury,

Massachusetts. Louise was many years younger than Alphonso. Her roots traced back to the Pilgrims.

Alphonso and Louise's first child, a boy named Sammie, died of whooping cough at the age of one. Will was their second child. After Will, the Tafts had three other children, Henry, Horace, and Fanny Louise.

Law and politics ran in the Taft family. Will's grandfather Peter was both a judge and a politician, having been elected to the Vermont state legislature. When Will was born, his father was a successful, well-respected attorney. Alphonso

Louise Taft and baby Will
──────── ✧ ────────

later served as secretary of war (a position now called secretary of defense), attorney general, and U.S. ambassador to Austria-Hungary and Russia.

Compared to the average family, the Tafts were doing very well—but they were not millionaires. Among rich people, the Tafts were not thought of as rich. Still, Alphonso was respected enough to become a top adviser to President Ulysses S. Grant. This was impressive, since most citizens with great power in the United States also had great wealth.

One thing separated the Tafts from other successful families in Cincinnati. Alphonso and Louise were not religious.

If asked, the family said they were Unitarian, a denomination that emphasizes reason and individual freedom of belief. But none of the family went to church regularly. At the time, most of the powerful, wealthy people in Cincinnati belonged to traditional Protestant churches, though the city did have Catholic and Jewish communities.

CINCINNATI KID

As a child, Will lived in a big house on the side of a hill. His neighborhood, called Mount Auburn, was on the outskirts of Cincinnati. In those days, Cincinnati was more like a group of villages than like the overcrowded cities in the Northeast. Mount Auburn was considered one of the city's nicest sections.

When Will was a child, Cincinnati was a relatively small city, surrounded by rolling green hills and lush vegetation.

The Taft children play in front of their house in 1868. Will is standing near the fence and his brother Henry is sitting on the pillar at left. Horace, Fanny, Louise, and their Aunt Delia are in the background.

———————————— ✧ ————————————

TAFT'S BIRTHPLACE

The house where Taft was born has been restored and turned into a museum in Cincinnati. Four rooms on the main floor of the William Howard Taft Historic Site have been made to look just as they did when Taft was a child growing up there. Museum exhibits highlight Taft's life and provide information about the many accomplishments of his children and grandchildren. A robot of Charles Taft, William's son, tells stories about various family members.

One thing Cincinnati had in common with larger cities was a less-than-friendly competition among different neighborhoods. Many fights broke out between Mount Auburn boys and those from other neighborhoods. The city's sections were referred to as hills, based on the hills upon which they were built. Residents lived on Mount Airy or Mount Adams or Mount Lookout.

"Which hill you from?" a tough kid might ask a stranger. But because he was tall and large, Will was not picked on very often.

ACTIVE CHILDHOOD

Will made it through childhood with only one major injury, but it was extremely serious. When he was nine years old, he was in a carriage accident while riding with his family. The carriage was going down a steep hill when something spooked the horses. The horses bolted and ran wild, and Will almost completely fell from the carriage. He was dragged down the street, his head bouncing off the bricks. He badly cut his head and fractured his skull. Fortunately, he recovered from his injuries.

As Will grew into his teen years, he grew taller and wider. He was nicknamed Big Lub. (The word *lubber* means "a big clumsy fellow," a term used affectionately in the Taft family.) Will's younger brother Henry was called Lub, and Horace was known as Little Lub. The youngest in the family, Will's sister Fanny, was spared a nickname.

Though heavy, Will was an athletic youth. During the summers, he swam in a nearby canal. His favorite sport was baseball. He was not a fast runner, but he played second base well. He threw the ball accurately, and with a bat in his hands, he earned a reputation as a good hitter.

Taft was also an excellent dancer. As a boy, he took ballroom dance lessons twice a week and was known for his graceful movements. And, with his blond hair and blue eyes, he looked good on the dance floor.

Besides being a skilled athlete and dancer, Will did well in school. At Woodward High School, he took college-level courses. He earned a reputation as an excellent writer, once composing a well-argued essay supporting women's right to vote. At the time, only men could vote in elections. Taft graduated from high school in 1874 at age sixteen. He was second

Will (seated, center) poses with his Woodward High School graduating class in 1874.

Will spent his entire life trying to live up to the high standards set by his father, Alphonso (right).

—————————— ✧

in his class, with a four-year grade point average of 91.5 out of 100.

This achievement didn't impress his father, who complained because Will wasn't first in his class. Throughout his childhood, Will had yearned for his father's approval. Alphonso was a successful man, and he demanded success in his children. Will tried hard to live up to his father's expectations. But rather than praising Will for his accomplishments, Alphonso asked him why he had not done better.

Will's father also accused him of being a procrastinator—a person who always puts off something that needs to be done. This was probably unfair, since Will always finished his schoolwork on time. At one point, however, Will complained to his brother Horace that no matter how hard he tried, he couldn't do anything very far in advance.

Just as his father had planned for him, young Will attended Yale College before enrolling in law school.

CHAPTER TWO

YALE MAN

Great things have happened and luck came my way, and I want to say that whatever credit is due of a personal character in the honor that came to me, I believe is due to Yale.

—William Howard Taft, March 18, 1909

As a youth, Will did not get to see his father very often. Alphonso often didn't get home from work until midnight or later. Nonetheless, Will felt his father's influence at every turn in his life. Alphonso assumed that Will, like all the Taft boys, would follow in his footsteps by attending Yale College in New Haven, Connecticut, and becoming a lawyer. And Will was eager to follow this plan.

Seventeen-year-old Will began his freshman year at Yale in the fall of 1874. He wrote to his father and described his busy schedule: "I begin to see how a fellow can work all the time and still not have perfect [marks]." Will waited until the last possible second to do tasks he did not want to do. For example, even if he had several weeks to complete a paper, he frequently put it off and wrote the whole thing in the hours before it was due.

He was under pressure to succeed at college, however. He had to compete with the reputation established by his half-brother Peter, who a few years earlier had set the record for the highest grades ever earned at Yale.

Following his father's advice, Will cut down on athletics. He needed more time to study than he had needed in high school. But he didn't stop playing sports altogether. When his father suggested that he join an intramural wrestling team, he again took his advice.

Will was known around Yale as a happy-go-lucky, good-humored young man. He did lose his temper occasionally, especially when students who didn't take school as seriously as he did interrupted his studying.

Even in his youth, Will had few bad habits. He didn't smoke. He had a glass of beer every once in a while but never drank heavily. He studied so much that he didn't have a chance to get in trouble.

MAKING CONNECTIONS

Once again following in his father's footsteps, Will joined the Skull and Bones Society, an exclusive fraternity, or social club, at Yale. Alphonso Taft had been one of the founders of the secretive fraternity. To be admitted, students had to apply and then be voted in by the members. Fraternity members, known as "Bonesmen," formed important social and business connections that served them later in life. As they moved into their careers, members looked out for each other in business and political matters.

The exclusive Skull and Bones Society met in this fraternity hall at Yale.

At least once during college, Taft veered from his father's influence. Alphonso was a strong supporter of the Republican Party and assumed that his sons would also join the Grand Old Party, as it is sometimes called. But in 1878, during a speech class, Will spoke highly of the Democratic Party, praising its support of states' rights, which, he said, kept the federal government from gaining too much power. But that was about the last time Taft spoke favorably of the Democrats. Largely through his father's influence, he became a Republican and stayed that way.

Although Will found his university classes challenging, he did not struggle. By the time he was a senior, he proved that his academic skills were superior. He graduated from Yale in 1878. Just as he had in high school, he finished second in his class.

YALE AND POLITICS: A TAFT TRADITION

William Taft's father, Alphonso, was the first Taft to attend Yale College *(above)*, which was renamed Yale University in 1887. All five of Alphonso's sons also went to Yale. William's older brothers Charles and Peter went on to law school after graduating from Yale. For a time, Alphonso had a private law practice with his two oldest sons as his partners. Charles was later elected to the U.S. Congress. Will's younger brothers Harry and Horace also attended Yale.

William Howard Taft remained connected to Yale even years after he left. In 1899 Taft was offered a job as president of the university, but he turned it down.

The family legacy continued into future generations. Both of William Taft's sons attended Yale. His oldest son, Robert, became a lawyer and went on to become a U.S. senator. Son Charles also practiced law and was later elected mayor of Cincinnati. One of Taft's grandsons also became a senator, and his great-grandson, Bob Taft, another Yale graduate, was elected governor of Ohio in 1999.

The Cincinnati Commercial
building, where Taft worked as a
reporter covering court cases
——————————— ✦

INTRO TO LAW AND POLITICS

After college Taft enrolled in Cincinnati Law School, which was considered one of the best law schools in the United States. Because there were few law schools at the time, many applicants were rejected. But Will had no trouble getting in, having proven himself an excellent student at Yale.

Classes at the law school were arranged to take up as little time as possible so students could also hold down full-time jobs. Classes took place in the morning and lasted no more than two hours a day. In the afternoons, Taft went to work. He took a job as a reporter for one of the city's daily newspapers, the *Cincinnati Commercial*. His assignment was to cover court cases.

Around this time, Will began to consider his ultimate goal in life. His dream was to become the top judge in the country—chief justice of the U.S. Supreme Court. For Will, as for his father and grandfather, serving as a judge was not just a job but a calling. In later years, Taft frequently compared being a judge to being a priest in a church—the church of justice. Serving on the highest court in the land, he felt, would be an honor and a joy.

Taft kept busy with work and school, but not so busy that he didn't have time for a social life. At a party in early 1879, he met a young woman named Helen Herron, who was called Nellie. Taft was twenty-one, and Nellie was eighteen. They liked each other right away. They even shared a bobsled ride down a hill. But they did not see each other again for another year, when he invited her to a get-together given by his brother Charles.

In the meantime, Taft's father was reaching the peak of his political career. In 1879 Alphonso Taft sought the Republican Party's nomination in the race for governor of Ohio. Four years earlier, he had tried and failed to win the nomination. His opponent this time was Charles Foster, a wealthy banker and railroad executive who had served four terms in Congress.

Taft entered the world of politics by campaigning for his father, hitting the streets of Cincinnati to work up voter support. He enjoyed the process but was not pleased with the outcome. Foster, with more political experience, won the nomination. After that, Alphonso never sought the nomination again.

In 1880 Will campaigned again, this time for city representatives in local elections. He talked to people about honest candidates who were trying to get crooked politicians out of office.

"I worked in my ward [section of the city] and some-times succeeded in defeating the regular gang candidate by hustling around among good people to get them out [to vote]," Taft said.

MAN OF ACTION

Taft received his law degree in 1880 and passed the Ohio bar exam, which gave him the right to practice law in the state. He was offered a job at the *Commercial* as a perma-nent reporter, but he turned it down. He told a friend that he covered court cases for the newspaper only to make himself a better lawyer. His goal had always been to have a career in law.

Taft started his first job as a lawyer in October 1880. He was appointed assistant prosecuting attorney for Hamilton County, Ohio. A prosecuting attorney, also referred to as a district attorney, represents the government in prosecuting, or trying, criminal cases in court. In crimi-nal cases, a law has been broken and a jury or judge decides if the person accused of breaking the law is guilty, and if so, what the punishment, or sentence, will be. The lawyer who represents the accused criminal is the defense attorney, while the prosecuting attorney represents the local, state, or federal government.

In Taft's first trial case, he prosecuted a cleaning woman who had stolen thirty-five dollars from her employer. The woman pleaded guilty, and Taft joined the defense lawyer in asking the judge for a light sentence. Taft did prosecute one murder case during his early days as Hamilton County's assis-tant prosecutor, but the jury acquitted the defendant (deliv-ered a not-guilty verdict) on grounds of insanity.

Taft's relationship with his father had not changed much. Around this time, Alphonso wrote to him, "I do not think that you accomplished this past year as much as you ought."

Taft's father underestimated him. Given the chance, Taft proved to be a man of action. During the fall of 1881, he encountered some young thugs who were throwing bricks through windows. When the police arrived, Taft helped them make the arrests.

In 1882 Taft received his first presidential appointment. The president of the United States, Chester A. Arthur, gave him a job as tax collector for the Cincinnati district. Taft was considered for the job, not because of his own accomplishments but because of his father's connections to the president. The year before, President Arthur had named Alphonso

——————— ✧

President Chester A. Arthur (right)
appointed Taft as Cincinnati tax
collector in 1882.

Taft as U.S. ambassador to Austria-Hungary, a prestigious and important position. Young Taft was in charge of making sure everyone in the Cincinnati area paid their taxes to the U.S. government.

PRACTICING LAW

By the end of the year, Taft was getting restless in his position as tax collector. The job was dull, and it simply wasn't what he wanted to do. Taft was anxious to restart his legal career. He wrote to President Arthur, asking him to accept his resignation. Taft agreed to stay on until his replacement could be named, so he ended up collecting taxes until March 1883.

Taft immediately went into private practice as a lawyer. He formed a partnership with Harlan Page Lloyd, a man twenty years his senior who had worked with Taft's father. Clients hired the law firm to represent their legal interests in a variety of situations.

During the summer of 1883, Will made his first journey outside the United States. He crossed the Atlantic Ocean on the steamship *Germanic* to visit his parents in Vienna, Austria, where Alphonso was serving as ambassador. Before crossing to the mainland of Europe, Will stopped in England, Scotland, and Ireland. Then, following a three-week stay with his parents, he went on a walking tour across Switzerland with a childhood friend. He did not get back to the United States until October.

THE CAMPBELL CASE

Taft gained fame around Ohio following a murder case in 1883. On Christmas Eve that year, two Cincinnati men had robbed and murdered their employer, a stable owner. One of the men was white and the other was black. People expected both of them to be hung, which was the punishment at the time for murder.

Although the black man was convicted of murder and hanged, the white man escaped the death sentence. Instead, the jury found him guilty of manslaughter, a lesser crime. The public was outraged. A crowd of 10,000 rioted for several days and burned down the Cincinnati courthouse.

——————————————— ✧ ———————————————

Nearly 10,000 citizens formed the mob that rioted and burned down the Cincinnati courthouse in early 1884. Bloody as well as destructive, the riot killed 56 people and wounded more than 200 others.

The white man's defense attorney, Tom Campbell, was an enemy of Taft. The two men did not like each other and had traded insults in the past. It was rumored that Campbell had tried to bribe (give money to) a juror in the case in exchange for the manslaughter verdict. As a result, the district court held hearings to determine whether Campbell should have his license to practice law taken away.

Taft played a key role in the Campbell hearings. When a senior lawyer on Taft's legal team became ill, Taft, as a last-minute substitution, gave the team's final argument. He spoke before the court for three hours, detailing every questionable acquittal Campbell had gained during his career as a defense attorney. The speech was so well received that Taft's name made the newspapers and he became widely recognized in public.

Although many people remembered Taft's name, far fewer recalled that, at the court hearing, Campbell was found not guilty. He was allowed to continue practicing law. Taft's reputation grew even though his side had lost the case.

PARTY POLITICS

In 1884 Taft campaigned for Republican James Blaine for president, but the Democratic candidate, Grover Cleveland, won the election. That year Taft was chief supervisor of the election in Cincinnati. He was in charge of preventing voters from cheating. He soon learned that there was no way to stop all the cheating. In Cincinnati in those days, corruption was rampant. Some people managed to vote more than once. People used the names of dead people to register to vote a second time. Voting booths recorded votes that were never made. Republicans and Democrats alike were guilty of trying to steal votes. Taft's deputies tried to keep their eyes on the Democrats but were largely ineffective. Republicans won the local elections nonetheless.

The Republican Party was only a generation old at the time. Formed in the 1850s by antislavery activists, it started as a third party, along with the Democratic Party—which had been founded in 1792 by Thomas Jefferson—and the Whig Party. In 1860 the Republican candidate, Abraham Lincoln, was elected president, and the Whig Party fell apart, leaving two major political parties.

During the 1880s, the Republican Party dominated the northern states, including Ohio, while the Democrats ruled the South. Despite their origins as the antislavery party, Republicans were unwilling to support further changes in the South that might have benefited African Americans. Democrats, on the other hand, favored equal rights, including the right to vote, for African Americans, many of whom had been freed from slavery only twenty years earlier.

The Republican Party was made up mainly of conservative farmers and manufacturers, although there was also a liberal wing of the party. The liberals wanted to pass laws that would help average citizens, such as workers and owners of small businesses. The conservatives favored big businesses and believed that the government should not interfere with business. The Democratic Party was known as the party of workers and immigrants.

A REPUTATION WORTH DEFENDING

In January 1885, Taft was appointed assistant county solicitor for Hamilton County. In this position, he worked with the county solicitor—the top law officer for Hamilton County—on civil cases. In civil cases, one party sues another party, in contrast to criminal cases, in which a person is accused of breaking a law.

By all accounts, Taft was an honest man. Anyone who dared to suggest otherwise provoked his temper. At the Republican National Convention in September 1885, an attendee was overheard saying that Taft was the sort of man who was willing to pay for votes. When Taft heard what had been said about him, he found the man and slapped him. No one was going to put a mark on Taft's clean reputation without a fight.

A few years after their first meeting, Taft began seeing the intelligent, ambitious Nellie Herron on a regular basis. They soon became close friends.

CHAPTER THREE

NELLIE

My greatest desire now is to write a book,
write it, I must confess, for money . . . because
I do so want to be independent.
—Nellie Herron, 1880

Taft hadn't forgotten about Nellie Herron, even though a year passed between their first and second meetings. He began seeing her more regularly in 1884, when he was invited to meetings that Nellie and her friends hosted in her living room. During these "salons," guests discussed books, poetry, philosophy, and history. Taft became a regular at the gatherings, and he and Nellie formed a friendship, occasionally going out together. Even after he had known her for three years, however, he still began his letters to her, "My dear Miss Herron."

"Miss Herron" was the daughter of a successful Cincinnati lawyer, John Williamson Herron. He had once been a law partner of Rutherford B. Hayes, who became president in

John Williamson Herron

———— ◇ ————

1877. Nellie's mother, Harriet Collins Herron, came from one of the city's most respected families. Nellie was one of eleven children. In those days, childhood illnesses claimed the lives of many children, and only eight of the Herron children had survived. Nellie was the fourth oldest.

Nellie was smart and ambitious. She wanted to see the world and accomplish things—and in the 1800s, one of the few ways for a woman to achieve such goals was to marry a successful man.

At age seventeen, Nellie had spent several weeks in the White House with her parents, as guests of President Hayes. During this visit, she dreamed of someday being First Lady, the wife of a U.S. president.

COURTING NELLIE

In 1885 the tone of Taft's letters to Nellie changed. It was clear that he had fallen in love with her. He began to court her, with an eye toward marriage.

In William Howard Taft, Nellie saw a man who was going places—maybe as far as the White House. She liked the fact that he didn't smoke and didn't drink to excess. He was absolutely trustworthy.

But she did not immediately let on to Taft how she felt about him. She did not show a strong interest at first. Taft wrote many letters to her, trying to win her affection. His letters were flowery and dramatic, even for the 1880s.

In one letter, Taft wrote, "I have walked the streets this morning with the hope of seeing you and with little other excuse. . . . You reflected a light, the light of your pure and noble mind over my whole life. With your sweet sympathetic nature you would strengthen me where I falter and make my family life a deep well from which I could draw the holier aspirations for a life of rectitude [moral honesty]."

Will proposed to Nellie for the first time in February 1885 but was quickly rejected. He made another try. And another. At the time, many well-to-do families considered it a sign of good breeding for a woman to refuse the first two or three marriage proposals. So Taft didn't give up until he got the answer he wanted. Nellie finally said yes in May.

WEDDING BELLS

The wedding was scheduled for thirteen months later, on June 19, 1886. It took place at Nellie's parents' house. According to the next day's newspapers, "The bride on this occasion was attired in a superbly-fashioned satin robe with embroidered front, and veil caught with sprays of white lilacs. A bouquet of sweet peas and lilies of the valley rested on her gloved hand."

The bridesmaids were Nellie's sister Maria and Taft's sister, Fanny. Will's brother Horace was the best man. After the three-hour wedding reception, Taft and his bride stopped at the Albemarle Hotel in Seabright, New Jersey, for a few days and then sailed to Europe. They spent much

Europe's beautiful and bustling cities, such as London (above),
were popular vacation spots for many wealthy people from
the United States in the late 1800s.

of the summer touring England, Scotland, and France.
They didn't get back to Cincinnati until the fall.

BACK TO WORK

Though Taft was doing well in his career, he was not rich.
He had to borrow money to pay for the house he had built
for Nellie and himself in the Walnut Hills neighborhood in
Cincinnati.

As the Tafts settled into married life, Nellie remained
active in society. She hosted many parties—some for fun,

some as "discussion groups"—and in turn she and Will were invited to many parties. She was interested in music, and not long after marrying Will, she became one of the organizers of the Cincinnati Philharmonic Orchestra.

Meanwhile, Taft's career continued to flourish. In March 1887, the governor of Ohio, J. B. Foraker, appointed Taft as judge in the Cincinnati Superior Court. Some people thought Taft was too young for the job. He was only twenty-nine years old.

Taft still tended to put off work that he didn't want to do. But as he approached his thirtieth birthday and a new job, he wrote to friends that he had come to a realization: he could no longer get away with procrastinating. By the time he started his new job, he was getting started on tasks the instant they were put before him.

This may not have been a "new" Taft but a happy Taft. He loved being a judge, so it was easy for him to do his work promptly. Later in life, when unpleasant tasks returned to his desk, his procrastination returned as well.

CHAPTER FOUR

JUDGE WILL

*I don't see that people with very modest incomes
don't live as happily as those who have fortunes.*
—William Howard Taft, 1891

One of the major social and political issues in the United
States in the late 1800s was workers' rights. At the time,
there was no minimum wage, no limit on the number of
hours people worked per week, and no restrictions on child
labor. (The minimum wage is the lowest hourly pay rate
that U.S. companies are legally allowed to pay their workers.) As a result, many laborers in the United States were
overworked, underpaid, and mistreated. If a worker was
fired and couldn't find another job, he or she faced starva-
tion. Older workers had no retirement pensions or social
security—if they wanted to retire, they had to rely on their
families to take care of them. Employers didn't provide
medical insurance, so workers who got sick and couldn't
afford treatment had to go without.

In an attempt to improve their situation, workers organized. Gaining strength in numbers, they formed unions of workers who agreed to go on strike—refuse to work—if their employers did not meet their demands. Business owners complained that they would go out of business if they paid the workers as much as they wanted.

Strikes divided the nation. Workers thought that their actions would lead to a better quality of life. Business managers believed that the strikes threatened the U.S. economic system of capitalism, in which companies were privately owned and owners were free to make decisions about how to run their businesses.

———————————— ✧ ————————————

Striking workers on the Illinois Central Line drive out an engineer who was trying to keep the trains running.

Some of the strikes affected the whole country. For example, in 1894 members of the American Railway Union went on strike. Without railroads, many businesses throughout the country could not function. Mobs of union protesters gathered in Chicago. When federal troops were called in to break up the mob, six union workers were killed.

As a judge, Taft had to preside over many cases involving disputes between workers and management. Like most people from well-to-do families, Taft was politically conservative on the subject of workers' rights. He supported unions' right to strike but was aware that strikes often led to violence and crimes. Taft believed in following the letter of the law and would not rule in favor of strikers who had broken laws. Although he was against the exploitation of laborers, especially children, Taft ruled on the side of the businesses in most labor disputes.

ANOTHER PROMOTION

After four years on the Superior Court, Taft received another promotion. In late 1889, President Benjamin Harrison appointed Taft as solicitor general. The solicitor general is the senior adviser to the attorney general, who is the top lawyer for the federal government. The solicitor general is the number two lawyer in the country.

This wasn't the only good news for the Tafts that year. During the summer of 1889, the Tafts' first child, Robert Alphonso Taft, was born.

Taft's new position was in Washington, D.C., the nation's capital. He reported for duty in February 1890. Nellie and the baby joined him later, after Taft found a house for the family.

Taft was a successful solicitor general, losing only
two of the cases he handled while in the position.

Taft was good at his new job, though he didn't find it particularly exciting. He helped determine the extent of the federal government's legal power. For example, did Congress have the right to overturn a trial conducted by the U.S. Army? No, according to Taft. Was it okay for Congress to prevent companies from cutting timber on government land? Yes. Of eighteen cases he handled as solicitor general, he lost only two. Taft was also learning valuable lessons about how Washington worked. Part of his job involved addressing the members of the Supreme Court—the court he hoped to serve on one day.

But Taft was convinced that he was a dull speaker and no one was listening to him. He complained, "I have difficulty in holding the attention of the Court. They seem to think when I begin to talk that that is a good chance to eat lunch, and to devote their attention to . . . other matters that have been delayed until my speech."

In May 1890, when the attorney general became ill, President Harrison named Taft as acting attorney general. Privately, Taft expressed doubts about his knowledge of the law and his public speaking ability. But in public, he appeared confident, and his career continued to move in only one direction—upward.

HOT WEATHER

Problems arose, however, when the summer heat arrived. Summers in Washington, D.C., could be brutal in those days before air conditioning. The heat was especially hard on Taft, who weighed more than three hundred pounds. Nellie and the baby escaped the heat at a summer home in Massachusetts, but Taft decided to tough it out. It was the one and only summer he ever spent in Washington.

Late in the year, Taft became concerned about his father as Alphonso's health began to slip. Taft wrote to his father daily during the first months of 1891, but Alphonso, suffering from lung ailments, grew weaker. He died on May 21, 1891.

Taft was devastated. Not only did he miss his father, but he feared that the "luck" his career had benefited from was about to run out. Taft didn't trust that his own abilities had anything to do with his success. He thought his father had been pulling strings for him.

As it turned out, Taft had nothing to worry about. His career success continued. And he and Nellie were lucky at home as well. On August 1, 1891, a daughter, Helen Herron Taft, was born.

CIRCUIT COURT

In March 1892, Taft was named a judge in the U.S. Sixth Circuit Court of Appeals (later renamed the U.S. Court of Appeals), a new court created by Congress to ease the crowded schedule of the federal courts. He was nominated for the position by a committee of Cincinnati lawyers and appointed by President Harrison. Taft served on the court for eight years. He and his family lived in Cincinnati during this time, but Taft traveled to hear cases in a wide area, including Kentucky, Michigan, and Tennessee.

Starting in the summer of 1892, the Tafts began a tradition of spending summers in Canada. They rented a cottage in Murray Bay on the Saint Lawrence River. Taft enjoyed these breaks. He ate well and relaxed. He liked to sit in an easy chair on his front porch and watch the river flow by.

Many of the circuit court cases had to do with large corporations and organized labor. The most important decision Taft made during his eight years on the court involved a monopoly case. A monopoly is exclusive control or ownership of a product or service, often gained by illegal methods of destroying fair business competition. Six pipe-making companies had gotten together and formed what is called a trust. They made an agreement to all charge the same price for the same goods. That way the companies could charge customers more than if they were competing with one another, since competition drives down prices. But when businesses form a trust, manufacturers who aren't part of the trust tend to be forced out of business since suppliers are afraid to sell to anyone outside the trust. Lawsuits and other actions to prevent business trusts are called "antitrust" actions.

In most antitrust cases he presided over, Taft ruled against the business trusts in favor of the squashed competitors. He said that companies needed to compete and should not be allowed to agree on prices in an attempt to put others out of business. However, when it came to labor strikes, which continued to be a source of conflict in the United States, Taft usually ruled against labor in favor of management.

In 1896 Taft became a dean and professor at Cincinnati Law School, where he had earned his law degree. He taught at the law school, and his students remembered him as a serious teacher with a lot of energy. The next year, on September 20, 1897, the Tafts' third and final child, Charles Phelps Taft, was born.

Nellie poses with the first two Taft children,
Robert (right) *and Helen* (left).

———————————— ◇ ————————————

A KEY FRIENDSHIP

During this time, Taft became increasingly close friends with Theodore Roosevelt. The two men had met several years earlier, when they were both working in Washington, D.C. They had lived in the same neighborhood, walked to work together, and frequently lunched together. At the time, Roosevelt was the civil service commissioner, in charge of managing "civil servants," or employees of the federal government.

Roosevelt remarked later, "You know, I think Taft has the most lovable personality I have ever come in contact with. . . . One loves him at first sight."

THEODORE ROOSEVELT

Theodore Roosevelt was born in New York City in 1858 into a wealthy family. He suffered from severe asthma as a child. As an adult, he became a symbol of vigorous activity.

In 1884, when Roosevelt was twenty-six years old, his first wife, Alice Lee Roosevelt, and his mother both died on the same day. To deal with his grief, he went to the Badlands in the Dakota Territory. Among other things, he drove cattle, hunted big game, and captured an outlaw. In 1886 Roosevelt returned to civilization. That year he married his second wife, Edith, and continued his career in public service (he had served on the New York state assembly in 1882.) Over the next several years, he held positions as civil service commissioner, police commissioner of New York City, and assistant secretary of the U.S. Navy.

Roosevelt became a household name during the Spanish-American War (1898) as leader of the First U.S. Volunteer Cavalry. Called the Rough Riders, the soldiers were the toughest horse riders Roosevelt could find. He led them on a famous charge at the Battle of San Juan, a high hill near Santiago, Cuba. The Rough Riders inflicted many casualties on the Spanish defenders and pushed them farther inland, where they soon surrendered.

✧ ————————

Theodore Roosevelt,
photographed in 1900

Roosevelt (far left in white uniform) *and his Rough Riders played a key role in the Spanish-American War.*

────────────── ◇ ──────────────

In 1898 Roosevelt ran as a Republican candidate for governor of New York and won. Two years later, presidential candidate William McKinley asked Roosevelt to be his running mate. Roosevelt accepted, and the team of McKinley and Roosevelt won the election. When McKinley was assassinated in 1901, Roosevelt became the twenty-sixth president of the United States. He was forty-two years old, the youngest president ever.

President Roosevelt moved the United States into world politics. He became known as a "trustbuster," breaking up monopolies to promote fair competition in business. Although he disliked being called Teddy, when the teddy bear was named after him, Roosevelt was smart enough to use the bear as a symbol in his next campaign.

In 1905 President Roosevelt led the peace talks that ended a war between Russia and Japan, and for this achievement, he won the Nobel Peace Prize in 1906. Under Roosevelt's leadership, many conservation programs were started to preserve forests and other public lands in the United States.

In 1896 Roosevelt was appointed assistant secretary of the navy by President William McKinley. Two years later, Roosevelt resigned from this position so he could fight in the Spanish-American War. The conflict centered on the fate of Cuba, an island off the southeastern coast of the United States. Cuba had long been ruled by Spain, but the Cuban people wanted independence. Many people in the United States demanded that the U.S. government help the Cubans. On February 15, 1898, the U.S. battleship *Maine* blew up in

President William McKinley
—————— ✧ ——————

the harbor near Havana, Cuba. Although it remains unclear what caused the explosion, the U.S. government assumed it was sabotage by the Spanish. In April the United States declared war on Spain. The war was short and one-sided, ending Spanish control of Cuba. As a result of the peace treaty, signed by the United States and Spain, Spain also gave the United States control of the Philippines, Guam, Puerto Rico, and other islands.

Taft did not even consider fighting in the war. Fighting might have helped his future political career, as it did for Roosevelt. But Taft did not envision a political career for himself. He was still dreaming of serving one day as a judge on the U.S. Supreme Court.

CHAPTER FIVE

GOVERNOR OF THE PHILIPPINES

We must have civil government here and must get rid of the one-man power.
—William Howard Taft, 1900

At the beginning of the twentieth century, the world was changing, and the United States wielded power and influence beyond the country's borders. Because of its abundant natural resources and leading role in the Industrial Revolution—the period of social and economic changes that transformed agricultural societies into industrial societies—the United States had become a world power.

This point was driven home to Taft in late January 1900 when he received a telegram from President William McKinley. Taft was surprised to learn that he had been named a member of a new commission to oversee the governing of the Philippine Islands. He had not previously given a thought to the Philippines.

The Philippines are a group of more than seven thousand islands south of Japan and Taiwan in the Pacific Ocean. The islands became a Spanish colony in 1565 and were named after King Philip of Spain. They remained under Spanish rule until the end of the Spanish-American War, when the United States acquired the Philippines as part of the 1898 treaty that ended the war.

When the United States took over the Philippines, the islands were in a state of rebellion. Many Filipinos wanted independence, but they did not have the structures in place for self-rule. Much of the population was poor, with little formal education. The economy in the islands was largely based on black markets (unregulated or illegal trade) and organized crime. In addition, many Filipino people were taken advantage of by the friars, members of several religious orders, or communities, within the Catholic Church. These Spanish religious men controlled many government functions, such as education, health, and taxes. The friars intimidated Filipino people into giving money and land to the Church.

President McKinley had sent seventy thousand U.S. troops to the Philippines to restore order, but the military effort had failed to squash the bloody rebellion. The disaster had embarrassed the president. He had to find another way to keep the peace in the Philippines.

WANTED: A GOOD GOVERNOR

The Philippines needed a good governor, and President McKinley believed that William Taft was the man for the job. Taft himself wasn't so sure. Seven different languages were spoken on the islands. He didn't even speak Spanish, the most common of the languages. He was also

afraid the appointment would stand in the way of his
career as a judge.

McKinley knew how to change Taft's mind. He was
aware of Taft's ultimate ambition. The president told Taft
that he would have a much better chance of serving on the
U.S. Supreme Court someday if he accepted this position
in the Philippines. That swayed Taft to accept the position.
He thought the job would last six months at most.

In the spring of 1900, the Tafts traveled to Asia. Taft
went directly to the Philippines, while Nellie and the children spent the summer in Japan, where it was cooler. Taft
arrived in the islands on June 3.

◇

The Tafts (center) *play cards on the deck*
of their boat en route to the Philippines.

General Arthur MacArthur (left) *and Taft did not agree about the best way to govern the Philippines.*
✧ ———————————

TROPICAL HEAT

Taft had trouble in the steamy intensity of the tropics. Temperatures in the Philippines were often over 90 degrees Fahrenheit, with high humidity. Taft developed rashes and skin infections from the heat.

Despite his discomfort, Taft set to work to learn as much as he could about the Philippines and start implementing basic improvements in government services, roads, and harbors. In Taft's view, the Filipinos were not ready to govern themselves, because they had been under Spanish rule for so long. But he also felt that they should be treated with dignity and given the greatest possible control over their own affairs.

His ideas clashed with those of General Arthur MacArthur, who commanded the seventy thousand U.S. troops that were stationed in the islands. (MacArthur was the father of General Douglas MacArthur, who would later command Allied forces in the Pacific during World War II (1939–1945).) General MacArthur believed that the Filipinos should be ruled with strict authority. He had troublemakers arrested and sent into exile on the Pacific island of Guam. When Taft arrived in the Philippines, however, MacArthur's power was greatly reduced.

The Tafts settled into their new home in Manila, the capital and largest city in the Philippines. Their house was known as the governor's palace. Nellie was pleased with her new living situation. The house was nicer than their home in Cincinnati, and she had many servants to help her manage the household.

One of the first things Taft did to reassure Filipinos of his intent to rule fairly was to make sure that local leaders were always invited to official meals at the governor's palace. Whenever possible, he treated the locals as equals. MacArthur was so angered by this that he was eventually transferred and replaced in 1901.

CHANGES AFOOT

One of Taft's first priorities was to set up an educational system for the islands. Some areas got schools for the first time. Older schools were modernized and better organized. Taft also set up local governments to help citizens learn how to build their own stable government. When Taft learned that the Filipino court system was corrupt, he fired the judges and replaced them with judges from the United States.

When Taft first arrived in the Philippines, many rural areas had no schools. These girls attended the Kabayan School on the Philippine island of Luzon.

———————————————— ✧ ————————————————

In November 1900, William McKinley was reelected U.S. president. This time his vice president was Taft's friend Theodore Roosevelt. In 1901 McKinley made Taft's office official. Taft was named civilian governor of the Philippines.

Taft's attempts to keep peace among the people of the Philippines were only partially successful. Many Filipinos wanted complete independence from foreign control. Filipino rebel fighters rioted and clashed with U.S. military troops, who were there to preserve U.S. rule. Other rebels fought against the friars, the Spanish religious men who had taken land from the Filipino people.

On September 6, 1901, President William McKinley was shot and killed by an assassin named Leon Czolgosz in Buffalo, New York. Theodore Roosevelt became the president.

TRIP TO ROME

In the Philippines, Taft also had to deal with the demands posed by the friars, who still controlled huge tracts of prime land in the islands and did not want to give up their power. Cruel and greedy, the friars often threatened Filipinos,

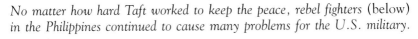

No matter how hard Taft worked to keep the peace, rebel fighters (below) in the Philippines continued to cause many problems for the U.S. military.

Taft met with Pope Leo XIII (left) in hopes of easing the control Catholic friars had on the Philippines.
✧ ——————————

telling them they would go to hell when they died if they didn't give their money to the Church.

Taft wrote to the pope, the head of the Catholic Church, in Rome for help with the situation. Taft asked Pope Leo XIII to order the corrupt friars in the Philippines to leave. In exchange, the United States would purchase at a good price all the land owned by the friars, land that belonged to the Catholic Church. President Roosevelt ordered Taft to travel to Rome to discuss the situation with the pope.

Taft took one steamship from the Philippines to the United States, then a second ship to Italy. The trip to Italy began during the spring of 1902. Nellie could not accompany her husband, because their son Robert was sick with scarlet fever. Taft's mother offered to travel with him instead.

In negotiations with Taft, the pope agreed to sell the land, but not to withdraw the friars. The friars stayed on, but their power had shrunk. The land they owned was gradually returned to the Filipinos.

Taft did not return to the Philippines until August 1903. While he was away, disease had devastated the Filipino people. Approximately 100,000 islanders had died from a disease called cholera. In addition to the widespread disease, a famine gripped the islands. Taft helped the situation by arranging for $3 million in relief money from the United States.

SANTO TAFT

During Taft's four years in the Philippines, he came to be widely trusted. He sincerely wanted what was best for the Filipinos. He didn't want just to control them. He wanted to lead them to freedom.

HOW IS THE HORSE?

During a goodwill mission to one of the Philippine Islands, Taft spent the day traveling by horseback through the mountains. He sent a telegram to U.S. secretary of war Elihu Root, briefing him on his day's activities.

"Stood trip well. Rode horseback twenty-five miles to five thousand feet elevation," Taft wrote.

The secretary of war envisioned the three-hundred-pound man and wrote back: "Referring to your telegram . . . how is the horse?"

Taft loved it. Showing his good sense of humor, he often told this story about the funniest telegram he ever received.

In 1903 six thousand people marched through the streets of Manila carrying signs. The signs read, "We Want Taft." The people referred to him as Santo Taft, or Saint Taft. When President Roosevelt wanted to send Taft a telegram, he addressed it simply, "Taft, Manila."

The Taft family had adjusted well to the Philippines. They had all learned at least some of the main local language, Filipino. This variety of a language called Tagalog was spoken on many islands in that part of the world. The children—ages thirteen, eleven, and five years old when they arrived—had made friends, and they had a deer, an orangutan, and a monkey as pets.

When Roosevelt twice offered to make Taft's dreams come true by appointing him to the Supreme Court of the United States, Taft had to turn down his friend. He told the president that his work in the Philippines was not yet done. The people were not ready to govern themselves. There was still too much crime, and the U.S. military was still clamping down too hard on the people.

Nellie approved of Taft's decision. She was not eager to see her husband sitting on the Supreme Court. She knew that a member of the Supreme Court is usually a member for life. If Taft accepted Roosevelt's offer, Nellie's dreams of being First Lady would be over.

She later wrote, "This was not a question which gave Mr. Taft even a shade of hesitation because he knew immediately what he must do. All his life his first ambition had been to attain the Supreme Bench. To him it meant the crown of the highest career that a man can seek, and he wanted it as strongly as a man can ever want anything. But now that the opportunity had come, acceptance was not to be thought of."

Hearing that Taft had turned him down, the president sent a telegram that read, "All right stay where you are. I shall appoint some one else to the Court. Roosevelt."

In the end, it was Taft's health, which would never be good as long as he remained in the tropics, that made him leave the islands for good in December 1903. Roosevelt appointed him the new secretary of war, convincing Taft to accept the position by pointing out that he would still have a hand in running the Philippines. He added, "If only there were three of you (for the Supreme Court, secretary of war, and governor of the Philippines)!"

The secretary of war was a member of the cabinet, the president's staff of top advisers. This meant that the Tafts would be returning to Washington, D.C. The move pleased Nellie. It put Taft back into the world of politics—right where she wanted him.

CHAPTER SIX

THE POLITICIAN

*I do not want my son to be president. His is a
judicial mind and he loves the law.*

—Louise Taft, William H. Taft's mother

Like Nellie, Taft thought the best part about his new cabinet position was that it put him back in Washington. He liked being where the action was, even though he was expected to give many speeches in support of Republican candidates and causes. Public speaking was never going to be Taft's favorite activity.

For one thing, he had to speak without the aid of microphones or public-address systems, which weren't invented yet. To be heard, Taft had to shout, and his voice was prone to hoarseness. Many people, hearing him speak for the first time, expected a deep, booming voice. But Taft had a surprisingly high-pitched voice.

Much of Taft's political work was in support of his friend President Roosevelt, who was elected to another term

in the White House in 1904. Although Taft's official position was secretary of war, Roosevelt did not need much
help running the military, so he relied on Taft to assist him
with a variety of tasks.

Roosevelt knew that Taft thrived on travel, so he never
hesitated to send him abroad to deal with a crisis in a foreign land. In 1905 Taft went to Japan to meet with the
Japanese premier, Count Taro Katsura, to help negotiate a
peace treaty between Japan and Russia.

When U.S. secretary of state John Milton Hay became
ill that year, Taft became the acting secretary of state. This
cabinet member oversees U.S. foreign policy. Hay died a
short time later, and Elihu Root became Roosevelt's new
secretary of state.

Taft was also put in charge of construction of the Panama
Canal. The United States had acquired a small piece of land in
Panama that extended from the Atlantic Ocean on the east to
the Pacific Ocean on the west, a
distance of fifty miles. This was
the spot where the Atlantic and
Pacific came closest together
between North America and
South America. A canal there

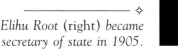

Elihu Root (right) *became*
secretary of state in 1905.

would allow ships to sail between the Atlantic and the Pacific
without having to make the long trip around Cape Horn, at
the southernmost tip of South America.

In 1906 Roosevelt called on Taft to help manage another international crisis—this time in Cuba. The treaty that
ended the Spanish-American War had made Cuba an independent nation, but the country was completely dependent
on the United States for its defense and its economy.
During the eight years since the war, the U.S. presence in
Cuba had failed to maintain law and order. A rebellion was
brewing. Taft began steps to form a new Cuban government, helping to avert a revolution.

THE PROGRESSIVE MOVEMENT

The Republican Party was a conservative group, made up
mainly of wealthy people who believed that the government
should not interfere with business. Theodore Roosevelt,
however, was not a typical Republican. He was aligned with
the Progressives, a political movement that thought big
business was growing out of control.

The Progressives worried that the rich were getting richer
and the poor were getting poorer. They believed that government owed it to the nation's citizens to end business corruption and halt the widening gap between rich and poor.
Progressives called for measures such as trust-busting, a graduated income tax—in which higher tax rates are applied to
higher incomes—and regulation of railroads. Several railroad
companies had formed alliances to keep prices artificially
high. Government regulation would help ensure honest competition, so the railroad companies would have to charge the
same or less money and provide better service.

THE PANAMA CANAL

The Panama Canal involved digging a fifty-mile-long ditch through a narrow, mountainous U.S.-controlled strip of land in Central America. With the canal, ships could get from the East to the West Coast of North America and back again without having to go all the way around South America. Taft visited the "Canal Zone" in 1904 *(below)* to help figure out how the canal should be built. He also wanted to convince the people of Panama that the canal was in their best interests as well as those of the United States.

Building the canal was a dangerous and grueling job. The "big ditch" had to be dug through thick jungle. Hundreds of workers came down with and died from serious illnesses such as yellow fever and malaria. Started by the French in 1881, the canal was not officially open to business until 1914.

Roosevelt intervened on the side of labor in strikes. He fought for women's right to vote and for equal treatment of both sexes in the workplace. His ideas made him very popular with the public and very unpopular with the businesspeople who represented the "old guard"—the older, more conservative members—of the Republican Party. The party put up with Roosevelt, however, because he was so popular with voters.

As Roosevelt's right-hand man, Taft was making enemies inside his own party. And since he was very conservative, he was supporting policies that he probably would not have considered on his own.

TEDDY AND NELLIE WEIGH IN

After the 1904 election, Roosevelt and Nellie Taft had a meeting of the minds. Early on, Roosevelt had decided that he was not going to run for a second term as president. He wanted to move on to other things—to have adventures while he was still young enough to pursue them. He had plans to go on safari in Africa, then write a book about the experience.

Roosevelt and Nellie agreed on one very important point: William Howard Taft would make a great next president of the United States. (Taft was not Roosevelt's first choice, however. Roosevelt wanted his assistant, former secretary of war Elihu Root, to succeed him. But Root did not want to run for president, so Taft ended up at the top of Roosevelt's list of possible successors.)

Up until the point when Roosevelt told Taft what he had in mind for Taft's future, Taft showed no signs of seeing it coming. Only days before Roosevelt proposed that

Taft run for president, Taft wrote in his journal, "I am very anxious to go on the Supreme Bench. The president has promised me a number of times that he would appoint me Chief Justice if a vacancy occurred in that position and he knows that I much prefer a judicial future to a political future."

As it turned out, what Taft preferred did not make any difference. He had told his wife many times that he didn't feel he had the proper personality to be president. He had used this argument when she first wanted him to go into politics. But Nellie was determined to steer her husband away from the Supreme Court and toward the White House. She even called family meetings—with everyone present except her husband—to discuss Taft's future.

Nellie got many family members to agree with her, but not Taft's mother. Louise felt strongly that it was a mistake for her son to go into politics because he did not have the personality for it.

Nellie won the battle of wills, and Taft finally gave in. In May 1906, Taft told Nellie, "I went to the White House for a long talk with the president. . . . He thinks I am the one to take his mantle [succeed him in the presidency]."

Taft didn't say yes right away, though. He told the president he would have to think about it. Roosevelt waited a couple of days and then called Nellie. He asked her to talk with her husband again and pressure him to agree. The two didn't relent until Taft gave in. Roosevelt told Taft that his decision was for the good of the country and it would make Nellie happy. One step at a time, Nellie's dream was coming true.

Nellie was instrumental in helping Roosevelt persuade Taft to run for the presidency. Without her constant pressure, Taft probably wouldn't have agreed to run.

——————— ✧

MAKING IT OFFICIAL

In 1906 Taft told his family that he would accept the Republican nomination for president in 1908, should it be offered. Roosevelt publicly announced his support of Taft with these words: "I believe with all my soul that Taft . . . represents the principles for which I stand. His policies, purposes, and ideals are the same as mine."

Many people felt that it wasn't right for a president to handpick the person he wanted to succeed him in office. But Roosevelt didn't care about that. Teddy was the most popular man in the land, and he easily would have been reelected if he had run. He felt he had a right to let people know his choice for the person to carry out his policies. He wasn't forcing anyone to vote for Taft. He was merely suggesting—and he was fairly certain that most voters would take the suggestion.

Roosevelt kept a close eye on Taft, making sure he didn't do or say anything that would hurt his chances of being elected. The newspapers began to portray Taft as Teddy's puppet, someone who simply echoed and agreed with everything the president said. T.A.F.T., the newspapers said, stood for "Take Advice From Theodore."

AROUND THE WORLD

In 1907 Roosevelt sent Taft on one last trip abroad. This time Taft's travels took him all the way around the world to meet with leaders of several nations. Taft did not want to go, because his aging mother was very ill. But Louise sent him on his way, telling him that no Taft had ever turned his back on duty because of personal troubles.

Taft traveled to Japan and the Philippines, then on to Europe for stops in Russia and Germany. In all, Taft visited eight countries and covered twenty-four thousand miles. On the way home, as he was crossing the Atlantic, he received a message saying that his mother had died at the age of eighty. Taft was saddened, but he also knew that she had lived a full life. When he returned to the United States, he went to Cincinnati and put a wreath on Louise's grave.

THE CAMPAIGN

As the 1908 presidential election approached, Roosevelt began to regret his decision not to run for another term. He enjoyed being president. And he was popular—the most popular U.S. president ever up until that point. He worried that he hadn't quite finished the job he had set out to do. He hoped Taft would continue his policies, but Roosevelt wasn't sure that Taft was up to the task.

The Republican Party convention took place that summer in Chicago. Right up until the moment that Taft won the party's nomination, many observers thought that Roosevelt was going to change his mind at the last second and seek reelection. But he kept his word and supported Taft.

Taft easily won the Republican nomination for president. He got many more votes than the other six candidates combined. The vice presidential candidate who won the nomination was James S. Sherman, a congressman from New York.

Nellie advised Taft to lose some weight for the campaign, so he went to Virginia and played golf for three months. He had never played the game before but quickly fell in love with it. Taft dreaded the campaign and all the speeches he would be required to make. He managed to avoid doing any campaigning at all until late September. The election was in the beginning of November. The Democratic candidate for president was William Jennings Bryan, who had twice before run for president—and twice lost. A former Nebraska congressman, Bryan believed that the United States should not control foreign countries such as the Philippines, and he supported their independence. Bryan also favored Prohibition (making it illegal to produce and sell alcoholic beverages), women's right to vote, and the income tax.

Taft's speeches during his campaign clearly showed his lack of enthusiasm for the presidency. In one campaign speech, Taft said, "The truth is, I am not much of a politician. I am from time to time oppressed with the sense that I am not the man who ought to have been selected, and yet, my friends, I am not going to decline."

He had been in no hurry to get off the golf course and hit the campaign trail. Much of the work was done for him

A handbill from the 1908 election
promotes Taft for the presidency.
————————— ✧

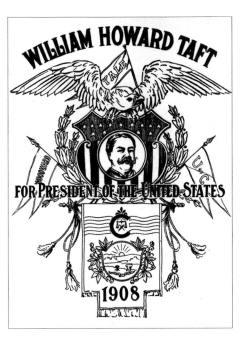

by President Roosevelt, who
gave speeches promoting
Taft as the man he had
chosen to replace him in
the White House.

During the campaign, Taft's size and his smile became
his trademarks. When Taft smiled, his cheeks and large
mustache rose and his eyes twinkled merrily. People in a
crowd or audience could easily see his smile, even from the
back row. Some of his supporters wore buttons that read,
"Smile, Smile, Smile." Everyone knew who those people
would be voting for.

In November Taft and Sherman won the election, with
51 percent of the vote. Bryan earned 43 percent. The
remaining 6 percent went to other candidates.

Nellie's dream had come true. She was going to be the
nation's First Lady. But for Taft, it was more like a nightmare than a dream.

*President Taft (center) and Vice President Sherman (right) stand
with the chief of the inaugural committee on Inauguration Day 1909.
A severe snowstorm delayed the ceremony.*

CHAPTER SEVEN

THE RELUCTANT PRESIDENT

*I hope that somebody, sometime, will recognize
the agony of spirit that I have undergone.*
—William Howard Taft, 1912

Between the election and the inauguration (the ceremony at which a new president is sworn in), Taft was filled with dread. He was convinced that he was destined to be a dismal failure as a president. Most men who reached the highest office in the nation were motivated by great political ambition and a desire to shape the country's future. But Taft did not want to be president. Although he agreed that it was for the best, his heart was not in it, and he doubted that he would live up to people's expectations.

The inauguration took place during a blizzard in March 1909. Taft quipped, "I always said it would be a cold day when I got to be president of the United States."

The weather was so bad that the inaugural parade had to march through six inches of slush on Pennsylvania

Avenue, the street that leads to the White House. Two spectators died of exposure to the cold. The colorful buntings—red, white, and blue flaglike decorations—that were hung everywhere to make the city look festive were ripped to shreds by the wind. Despite the foul weather, Nellie Taft, normally not an emotional woman, burst into tears of happiness moments after her husband took the oath of office and officially became president.

On that day, Nellie became the first First Lady to ride beside her husband during the inaugural parade. Previously, the outgoing president had ridden with the new one, and the departing and incoming first ladies rode together

———————————————— ◇ ————————————————

Nellie was overjoyed when Taft became president. Despite public disapproval, she proudly rode at his side during the inaugural parade.

behind their husbands. Roosevelt, however, decided not to compete with Taft on his day, so he was not in the parade. That left an opening next to Taft. Nellie didn't care if other people thought it was improper for her to ride with the president. She saw disapproval on the faces of some parade watchers, but this only made her more determined to be at her husband's side.

Besides Taft himself, Roosevelt was one of the first people to realize that the new president was not exactly going to take to his job like a fish to water. During the early days of the Taft administration, when all was seemingly going well, Roosevelt foresaw trouble. The former president said, "Taft means well and he'll do his best. But he's weak. They'll get him. They'll lean against him." Roosevelt realized, a bit too late, that Taft was not a natural leader.

GETTING TO WORK

Taft was not on the job in the White House for long before he realized there was a lot more work than he had counted on. And much of it was work he did not relish. His childhood habit of putting off tasks that he did not care for returned. He fell behind in his work and never caught up—although his critics were quick to note that he always seemed to have time to play a round of golf or attend a party. Taft once caused a small furor when he refused to meet with the president of Chile, who had just arrived in the United States, because he had a golf game planned.

Although Taft may have preferred to play golf, he did have some achievements as president. For example, he made

Golfing provided momentary relief from the pressures of the difficult job of president, which Taft had never wanted.

✧ ————————————

changes to improve conditions for workers. He saw to it that government workers no longer had to work more than eight hours a day. Over the years, serving as a judge in cases involving unions and strikes, Taft had grown more sympathetic toward laborers. While Taft was president, laws were passed that improved job safety for railroad and mine workers. Owners of rail and mining companies balked at spending money for safety devices, even something as simple as goggles to protect workers' eyes. Many railroad workers were injured or killed when devices that helped trains switch or cross tracks did not function properly. Mine workers were injured or killed when cables designed to lift and lower men into the mines operated for years without being replaced. Taft helped institute safety standards, including frequent inspections of equipment.

He also fought for workers' compensation. At the time, the law said that laborers who were injured on the job were not entitled to compensation for their injuries if they knew of the dangers when they took the job. This "assumed risk" rule allowed employers to ignore safety hazards.

As president, Taft established a federal bureau to deal with the problem of child labor. At the beginning of the twentieth century, one-third of all industrial workers were children. Taft appointed Julia Lathrop to head the new Children's Bureau of the Labor Department. This was the first step toward the enactment of laws regulating child labor. And Lathrop was the first woman ever appointed to head a government agency.

Taft also continued his antitrust policies as president. Theodore Roosevelt is commonly thought of as the leading trustbuster of the early twentieth century. But Taft, working through his attorney general, George Wickersham, initiated twice as many antitrust lawsuits as Roosevelt had during his presidency.

Taft also vowed to do something to improve the way black people were treated in the United States. In the early twentieth century, African Americans

——————— ✧
As chief of the Children's Bureau, Julia Lathrop also helped women understand the importance of infant and child health care in reducing sickness and premature death.

were still considered second-class citizens. In the South, conditions for blacks were only slightly better than they had been during the days of slavery. The Supreme Court ruled in the late 1800s that segregation, or separation of the races, was legal. In southern states, blacks and whites used separate public facilities, including schools, restrooms, restaurants, and sections on trains. As a result, many blacks began to move to northern cities, where they sought greater opportunities. Organizations such as the National Association for the Advancement of Colored People (NAACP) and the National Urban League were formed during the Taft administration to advocate for civil rights for African Americans.

Taft tried to set an example for other white employers by hiring African Americans whenever he could. He was the first president to hire black security guards to work in the White House. Taft once wrote to his wife that he had tried to secure more jobs for African

✧ ————————

NAACP founder W. E. B Du Bois created the Crisis magazine in 1910 as a forum for discussing civil rights issues.

Americans in government but had found it difficult: "The prejudice against them is so strong that it makes few places available, and yet I must do something for the race, for they are entitled to recognition."

TARIFF TROUBLE

One of the biggest problems President Taft faced involved tariffs (taxes) on goods imported into the United States. U.S. producers, who feared competition from overseas, wanted the tariffs to be as high as possible. High tariffs raise the price of imported products and encourage buyers to purchase lower-priced goods made in the United States. As Taft took office, tariffs were at an all-time high.

Previous presidents, with the exception of Grover Cleveland, had ignored tariffs, sensing that the issue was a political nightmare. Cleveland had attempted tariff reform in 1887 but failed. Taft supported lowering tariffs somewhat so that more U.S. citizens could afford to buy imported goods. He also wanted the United States to be part of the world economy. Some liberal politicians pushed for very low tariffs, without concern for U.S. businesses. Taft hated this kind of thinking, but because he supported lower tariffs, he was often labeled a liberal.

Speaker of the House Joseph G. Cannon—the top leader in the House of Representatives and Taft's political enemy—opposed any reduction in tariffs. Congress resisted Taft's moves to lower tariffs. Taft ordered a special session of Congress in 1909 to deal with the issue. The bill that was finally passed on August 5, 1909, the Payne-Aldrich Tariff Act, was a compromise. Tariffs were raised on some items and lowered on others. The new rules didn't make anyone happy,

TRIMMING THE PAMPERED DARLING.
Mr. Taft.—Stop licking! I might cut your head off!

This political cartoon suggests that high tariffs, which Taft wanted to trim, benefitted only the wealthy. Taft's ideas to lower tariffs were met with sharp criticism.

✧ ————————————

and the U.S. tariff system didn't change very much as a result of the legislation. Taft's action demonstrated his stubbornness on the subject more than his effectiveness.

Taft boasted that the tariff bill was the best piece of legislation the Republicans had ever passed. The press twisted these words to make it seem like Taft had changed his opinion and was in favor of even higher tariffs. Taft's message was lost. Throughout his presidency, his inability to deal with the press put him at a disadvantage in selling his ideas to the public.

DOLLAR DIPLOMACY

Another way Taft tried to transform the United States into a world power was by supporting U.S. business interests around the world. Many companies based in the United States owned factories, plants, and other operations in foreign countries. U.S. companies also sold goods to other countries. Some of these foreign nations were struggling to maintain stable governments. Taft feared that if the foreign governments collapsed, U.S. business interests would be threatened. He encouraged U.S. investment in these countries as a way to promote stability and order.

This effort to achieve foreign policy goals through economic means became known as "dollar diplomacy." It included measures such as paying off debts in Haiti and Nicaragua and financing the construction of a major railway in China. Taft was accused of trying to buy the friendship of foreign countries. He replied that it was better to use dollars than bullets.

Dollar diplomacy did not always work. In some countries, including China, Mexico, and the Dominican Republic, revolutions took place despite the influx of U.S. money, upsetting both diplomatic and business relations between those countries and the United States.

ILLNESS AND TRAVEL

Taft's days in the White House were darkened when Nellie Taft had a stroke in May 1909. She collapsed while bringing her eleven-year-old son Charles to the hospital for an operation on his adenoids (tissues in the upper throat that are similar to the tonsils). She recovered, but her speech was affected. She slurred her words for some time after her stroke and was unable to carry out her duties as White House hostess. The Tafts' nineteen-year-old daughter, Helen, often took her place.

Later that year, sensing that his popularity was waning, Taft decided to get away from Washington and, as he put it, "jolly" the American people. He wanted to take advantage of the power of his physical presence and easy-going

Helen Taft took over hostess duties at the White House at the age of nineteen.

personality to improve his standing in the public. He set out on a thirteen-thousand-mile trip, crisscrossing the United States from coast to coast. He even crossed the border into Juárez, Mexico, where he had a meeting with Mexican president Porfirio Díaz.

Some of Taft's aides expressed concern about his safety. It had only been a decade since President McKinley's assassination. But Taft refused to worry. He said that if people wanted to shoot him, they could. After all, he joked, he was such a big target. The last part of Taft's trip was a boat ride down the Mississippi River from St. Louis, Missouri, to New Orleans, Louisiana.

THE TAFT WHITE HOUSE

During Taft's lifetime, the United States was sprinting into the modern world. Taft was the first U.S. president to drive an automobile. And he wasn't content to drive around the streets of Washington at seven miles per hour. He liked to take his car into the Maryland countryside and drive fast. This, the president explained, helped to relax him.

Taft had the horse stables at the White House converted into garages for his cars. He had four automobiles, different models all made by the Ford Motor Company.

Some historians suggest that Taft felt trapped inside the White House. For much of the second half of his term he traveled, and when he was in the White House, he enjoyed sneaking out on his own. Once, pleased as a boy playing hooky from school, he bragged that he had made it seven blocks from the White House before anyone recognized him.

Taft's long trips gave him a good excuse not to keep up with his daily work. When he traveled, he brought along his own personal chef, so that he would always eat well. He was never heavier than when he was president.

In fact, Taft was the heaviest president ever. He quickly discovered that the White House bathtub was too small for him. Soon after moving in, he had a new bathtub installed to fit his size. He also had a special car with an extra wide door so he could get in and out more easily.

During Nellie's time in the White House, she also made some changes in and around the presidential residence. She had three thousand cherry trees planted along the rim of the nearby Tidal Basin, a lake that had been created from

———————————— ✧ ————————————

Nellie Taft was responsible for the cherry trees planted along the Tidal Basin. They create a spectacular sight each spring when they blossom, and many people travel to Washington, D.C., just to view them in full bloom.

*The Tafts' milk cow, Pauline Wayne, grazes outside the State,
War, and Navy Building in Washington, D.C.*

part of the Potomac River. The trees were a gift from a
Japanese chemist and presented to Nellie by the wife of the
Japanese ambassador.

Taft was the last president to keep a dairy cow on the
White House grounds. The cow's name was Pauline Wayne.
Not only did she supply milk for the Tafts, but by grazing,
she kept the presidential lawn short as well.

While Taft was president, he and his family had to tem-
porarily discontinue their tradition of spending summers in
Canada. Instead, they moved to the coastal town of Beverly,
Massachusetts, for the summer, staying in a house that
became known as the "Summer White House."

CHAPTER EIGHT

MORE WHITE HOUSE TROUBLES

I do not know much about politics but I am trying to do the best I can with this administration until the time shall come for me to turn it over to somebody else.
—William Howard Taft, 1910

In 1910 Taft's presidency became bogged down in a scandal. At the time, vast amounts of land in the United States were still undeveloped. During the previous administration, President Roosevelt had wanted to maintain open space and protect the country's natural resources. He made thousands of acres of land unavailable for development—the land was off-limits to any private homes or businesses. Taft's problems began when his secretary of the interior, Richard Ballinger, was accused of taking some of this land away from the government to give to oil companies. Ballinger was in charge of the Department of the Interior, the nation's principal conservation agency. This agency works to preserve (conserve) and protect natural resources such as land, water, fish, and wildlife, as well as energy and mineral resources. (*Conservation* refers to the preservation and management of natural resources.)

The accusation against Ballinger was made by Louis Glavis, an agent of the Interior Department. It was backed up by the head of the U.S. Forest Service, Gifford Pinchot, who had been appointed by Roosevelt. Pinchot claimed that Ballinger and the Interior Department had abandoned Roosevelt's policies.

——————————————— ◇ ———————————————

Gifford Pinchot (left) *bitterly accused Richard Ballinger* (right) *of abandoning Roosevelt's conservation policies.*

Taft reviewed the accusations and concluded that Ballinger had done nothing wrong. But Pinchot wouldn't back down, and nationwide attention was soon focused on the controversy. After trying unsuccessfully to calm Pinchot and Ballinger, Taft fired Pinchot. The move was seen as a rejection of Theodore Roosevelt's commitment to conservation of undeveloped land.

Ballinger, angered at the charges, demanded that Taft call for a congressional investigation into the matter. The investigating committee found Ballinger innocent of any wrongdoing, but his reputation suffered anyway. Ballinger resigned in March 1911, citing poor health.

The Ballinger-Pinchot affair did nothing to help Taft's popularity. The newspapers savagely attacked him throughout the ordeal.

Taft still thought of himself as a popular president. Crowds laughed when

---

ARGUMENTS OF COUNSEL.

FRIDAY, MAY 27, 1910.

JOINT COMMITTEE TO INVESTIGATE THE
INTERIOR DEPARTMENT AND FORESTRY SERVICE,
Washington, D. C., May 27, 1910.

Mr. BRANDEIS. Are we now ready to proceed?
The CHAIRMAN. Yes.

OPENING ARGUMENT OF LOUIS D. BRANDEIS.

Mr. BRANDEIS. Mr. Chairman and gentlemen of the committee, a great mass of evidence has been submitted to you at these hearings and a large number of subjects have been touched upon; some of them bearing on the fundamental conception of democracy, bearing on the demands of truth, of loyalty, and of justice. But whatever subject was touched upon, practically the center to which all testimony was directed has been the conduct of Mr. Ballinger, his acts, and his omissions. And in connection with that testimony much has been said and much evidence has been introduced, which, in our opinion, subjects him to severe criticism. Some of you undoubtedly will not agree with us as to the extent to which that criticism is justified; but I take it that the main issue which you have to consider is one on which men who have heard this testimony ought not to differ—because the main issue is this:

Is the Department of the Interior, as Glavis phrased it, in safe hands?

Or, to put it in other words, Has the conduct of Mr. Ballinger been such, is his character such, are his associations such that he may safely be continued as trustee for the people of their vast public domain, that he may be continued as manager of the reclamation and other kindred services, that he may be safely relied upon to represent the people in that great and sacred trust?

Or, to put it in still other words, Is Mr. Ballinger a man, single minded, able, enlightened, so zealous in the protection of the interests of the common people, so vigilant, so resolute, that he may be relied upon to protect the public domain, their great assets, upon which the welfare of the present and future generations of American people so largely depend; may he be relied upon to protect all that against the insidious aggressions of special interests who are ever looking for opportunity to seize upon that which is the property and the hope of the American people? Is Mr. Ballinger, in other words, the man to be the trustee of all this for the common people?

We submit, Mr. Chairman and gentlemen, that whatever differences there may be in the committee as to the degree of culpability of Mr. Ballinger for particular acts or omissions, there ought not

4903

✦ ————————

Taft appointed a committee to look into the Ballinger-Pinchot affair. At left is a transcript from one of the committee's hearings.

he laughed, and people seemed to like him. He mistook his personal popularity for the popularity of his policies. Adding to Taft's inability to judge his own popularity was the fact that he surrounded himself with people who tended to filter out bad news. Cabinet members knew that Taft would sulk and become inactive when criticized, so they kept things cheery.

TEDDY TROUBLE

While Taft struggled as president, Theodore Roosevelt was on a long safari in Africa. When Roosevelt returned to the United States in June 1910, he found the Republican Party in chaos. Roosevelt supporters within the party were very unhappy both with Taft and with the conservative wing of the party. The press said that Taft was a friend of rich businessmen, but the business owners themselves disagreed. Hadn't he battled them on the tariff bill?

Upon his return, Roosevelt completely turned on his friend. He was upset that Taft, who had promised to keep Roosevelt's cabinet in place, had instead replaced all but two of his men. He was angry that Forest Service chief Gifford Pinchot had been fired because of the Ballinger scandal.

The differences between Roosevelt and Taft seemed more glaring than ever. Roosevelt believed that a jury should have the right to overthrow a judge's decision. This appalled Taft, who lived according to the orderly rules of the law and believed that judges should have more power than juries. Roosevelt, on the other hand, disliked rules in general. He was willing to push them aside if they got in the way of what he thought was right.

Baseball and Presidents

The seventh-inning stretch was not Taft's only contribution to
baseball history. He also invented the ceremonial first pitch at
the same game, the season opener on April 14, 1910.

An announcer introduced the team managers to the
crowd, then acknowledged the president. Taft *(above, center)*
waved to the crowd. Umpire Billy Evans handed Taft the
baseball and asked him to throw one over home plate.

Taft—an old ballplayer—was glad to do it. He tossed the
ball to the Washington Senators' pitcher, Walter Johnson.

The crowd loved it. And so a tradition began for the
president of the United States to open each baseball season
with the first pitch. The "ceremonial first pitch" has since

expanded to other baseball games, especially in the World Series. Someone famous throws a ball to the catcher, the catcher gives the ball back to the celebrity, and the pair are photographed together.

Taft was not the only president who enjoyed America's favorite sport. Presidents and baseball have frequently been associated. George Washington and his soldiers played an early version of baseball called "rounder" at Valley Forge in 1778. John Adams, president from 1797 to 1801, enjoyed a game that he called "bat and ball." In the 1820s, Andrew Jackson played a baseball-like game called "one old cat."

Abraham Lincoln was a well-known baseball fan—so much so that an 1860 cartoon showed him playing baseball against his political opponents. Andrew Johnson gave his staff the day off one spring in 1867 so they could go to a ball game. During Johnson's presidency, in the late 1860s, baseball was played at the White Lot, an open area between the South Lawn of the White House and the current location of the Washington Monument. People still play softball in that area, later renamed the Ellipse.

Benjamin Harrison was the first president to attend a major-league baseball game when he saw Cincinnati beat Washington on June 6, 1892. The National League was playing its sixteenth season at the time.

President Ronald Reagan was a baseball announcer as a young man in the early 1930s, and as a movie actor, he played Hall of Fame pitcher Grover Cleveland Alexander in the 1952 movie *The Winning Team*. Before George W. Bush became president, he was an owner of the Texas Rangers baseball team from 1989 to 1994.

When Roosevelt talked about Taft's presidency, he noted how much better he himself would be doing at the job if he were in office. He would have gotten a real tariff bill passed, Roosevelt claimed. Rather than supporting the president, Roosevelt undercut Taft.

Taft was deeply hurt by this betrayal by his close friend. In response to one of Roosevelt's criticisms, Taft said, "It is hard, very hard, to see a devoted friendship going to pieces."

———————————— ◇ ————————————

This cartoon ultimately blames Roosevelt for burdening the Republican Party (the elephant) with Taft and his policies.

In 1910 Edward Douglas White became the oldest chief justice ever appointed to the Supreme Court.

NEW CHIEF JUSTICE

While Taft was president, he had the opportunity to name the new chief justice of the Supreme Court. This was the job he himself had always dreamed of holding.

The appointment posed a dilemma for Taft. He had always said that a new chief justice should be young enough to put in ten or twenty years of service on the Court. The problem was, if he appointed a young man for the position, Taft might never have an opportunity to serve on the Court. If he appointed an older man, Taft would increase his own chances of serving one day.

In December 1910, Taft appointed Edward Douglas White, who was sixty-six years old—six years older than any other chief justice had been at the time of his appointment. White was also the first chief justice to belong to a different political party (Democrat) and religion (Roman Catholic) than the president who appointed him.

TOO MANY APOLOGIES

Taft's lack of leadership and inability to get things done led to criticism from the press and other politicians. One by one, he began to lose political allies. Most successful politicians find a way of saying things so that all parties think they got what they wanted. Taft did not have this skill. He tended to say what he meant without regard to what people would think.

Taft didn't try to defend himself from attacks by his political enemies or the press. When a newspaper editorial said that Taft was a bad president, he apologized. He told his critics that they would not have to wait long until there was someone in the White House whom they liked better.

When Taft became angry with reporters, he stopped speaking to them. In an almost childlike way, he would go someplace where he could be alone and sulk. All presidents face criticism and make some political enemies, but Taft never came to grips with this reality.

Taft's presidency was further weakened when he allowed himself to be photographed standing next to his political rival, Speaker of the House Joseph G. Cannon. While sharing a podium with Cannon, Taft even referred to him by his nickname, "Uncle Joe." The photos in the newspapers, along with Taft's friendly words, sent a message that Taft had not intended. The stories made it seem as if Taft had turned his back on his friends and was siding with the opposition. Taft's supporters were outraged. Another of Taft's shortcomings was that he had trouble remembering people's names, even the names of supporters he was supposed to know.

By 1911 Taft was starting to think of himself as a one-term president. "I am not thinking of being re-elected in 1912," he said. "In fact, I don't know if I care for a nomination."

*Many Republicans felt that Taft deserved a second term in office,
as reflected in billboards posted in Ohio and other states.*

─────────── ✧ ───────────

THREE-WAY RACE

After Roosevelt turned against Taft, the two were never
friends again. Although Taft was not happy as president, he
agreed to run for reelection because he believed that his
party needed him. Many Republicans feared Roosevelt,
whose policies were becoming increasingly liberal. Party
leaders told Taft that Roosevelt was certain to win the
Republican nomination for president if Taft did not run.
As a loyal Republican, Taft agreed to do so.

Both Roosevelt and Taft ran for the Republican nomination, and Taft won. It is customary for candidates who
fail to win their party's nomination to support the winner

in the presidential campaign. But Roosevelt did not do this. Instead, he and his followers quit the Republican Party in protest over Taft's nomination. They formed their own party, the Progressive Party, which became better known as the Bull Moose Party. The name "Bull Moose" stemmed from a remark Roosevelt had made when a reporter asked how he felt. "I feel as strong as a bull moose," Roosevelt said.

In the election in November 1912, the Republican vote was split between Taft and Roosevelt. As a result, the Democratic candidate, Woodrow Wilson, easily became the next president. Taft finished third in the election. He still holds the record for the fewest votes received by a sitting president in a bid for reelection.

TAFT'S LEGACY AS PRESIDENT

During his lifetime, Taft was not thought of as a good president. He did not consider himself an effective leader, and the written record of the time is critical of his administration. While he was in office, he was sometimes referred to as "Taft the Blunderer." However, Taft did have some successes, although he rarely bragged about his accomplishments. He established the Bureau of Mines to make conditions safer for mine workers. He set up a federal office to regulate child labor. He instituted safety rules and benefits for rail workers, and in 1912 he oversaw the admission of two new states, New Mexico and Arizona, into the United States.

During the last months of his presidency, Taft submitted an amendment to the Constitution that would allow the federal government to collect income tax. Taft was not a strong supporter of the idea. The income tax had been a part of the Democratic Party's platform (policies) for years, but it was not popular with Republicans. When Taft put the amendment to the states for a vote, he was fairly certain that a popular vote would kill the idea. But that's not what happened. The Sixteenth Amendment was ratified in 1913, and the income tax has been a part of life in the United States ever since.

When it came time for the Tafts to leave the White House in January 1913, Taft left with a sincere smile on his face. At fifty-five years old, he was looking forward to getting on with his life.

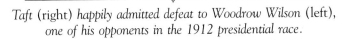

Taft (right) *happily admitted defeat to Woodrow Wilson* (left), *one of his opponents in the 1912 presidential race.*

Though Taft was a weak president, he relished his job on the Supreme Court, accomplishing much during his eight years as chief justice.

CHAPTER NINE

FINALLY, THE SUPREME COURT

I love judges and I love courts. They are my ideals; they typify on Earth what we shall meet hereafter in heaven under a just God.
—William Howard Taft, 1921

"You don't know how much fun it is to sit back . . . and watch the playing of the game [politics] down there in Washington, without any responsibility of my own," said Taft. The former president was relieved to have his years in the White House behind him.

Not long after his presidency ended, Taft took a job as a professor of constitutional law at Yale University. He lectured between four and eight hours a week. The job paid five thousand dollars per year—a sharp drop from his salary of seventy-five thousand a year as president. But he was more than happy to take a pay cut. For the next nine years, he taught classes, coached the freshman debating team, and wrote books. During the summers, when he didn't have to teach, Taft played golf in the cool air of Canada.

One of the books Taft wrote, *Our Chief Magistrate and His Powers*, about the presidency, became a well-respected work. He also wrote *Four Aspects of Civic Duty,* and five volumes of his speeches and other writings were published.

Taft was not the only member of the family to achieve literary success. Nellie also wrote a memoir, called *Recollections of Full Years,* which was published in 1914. In addition to writing, the former First Lady, who was once again healthy, earned up to one thousand dollars per speech for giving talks on subjects such as the duties of citizenship.

The Tafts continued to be a close family. Taft and Nellie often vacationed with their children in the

——————————— ◇ ———————————

The Tafts pose for a family portrait in 1911. Seated are Nellie and William Taft. Standing in the back are their children, Charles, Helen, and Robert.

summer. Their son Robert graduated from Harvard University Law School in 1913 and, like his father, became a lawyer. Son Charles, the baby of the family, also chose the family profession.

LOSING WEIGHT

During these years, Taft was very happy, and he was finally able to stay on a diet. He lost 80 pounds, dropping from 350 to 270. Because of the weight loss, Taft no longer needed his valet, the man who helped him get dressed and undressed. He could change his clothes by himself.

In 1917 the United States entered World War I (1914-1918), a conflict that had started in Europe in 1914 and gradually involved many nations. Taft reentered public life during the war when he accepted a post as joint chairperson of the National War Labor Board, which decided disputes between labor and management. Taft showed much more sympathy toward laborers during this period than he had in the past.

Taft and Roosevelt never became friends again after their disputes during Taft's presidency, but they did stop being enemies. They found a common cause in politics and reunited for campaigning purposes. They were on polite terms when Roosevelt died in January 1919.

ONE DREAM LEFT

For eight years, Taft had no chance to be nominated to the Supreme Court, which was his ultimate ambition. He would need to be appointed by the president, and Democrat Woodrow Wilson was not likely to do so.

But the outlook brightened in 1920, when a Republican, Warren G. Harding, was elected president. In 1921 Chief Justice Edward White died. Taft began a full-time campaign to make sure President Harding knew that he was available for the job.

He wrote letters. His friends wrote letters. He persuaded newspapers across the country to publish editorials stating that former president William Howard Taft should be appointed chief justice. Harding got the hint and nominated Taft for the job. Taft's lifelong dream finally came true. Not only would he serve on the court that he had called the "root of the tree of our civilization," but he would be its head judge.

Taft was sixty-four years old when he became the tenth chief justice of the United States Supreme Court on June 30, 1921. He had been thinking about serving on the

✧ ————————
Warren G. Harding (left) made Taft's lifelong dream come true when he appointed him to the Supreme Court in 1921.

highest court in the land for his entire life, and he did not waste any of his time there.

GRABBING THE BULL BY THE HORNS

Taft quickly became one of the most effective chief justices in history. He worked very hard. During the time he served as chief justice, he wrote one of every five of the Court's opinions—253 opinions in all. (A court opinion is a formal document explaining the legal principles that guide the ruling, or decision, in a case.)

In 1925 Taft was instrumental in helping win the passage of a bill in Congress that completely reorganized the federal court system. The new legislation, informally known as the Judges' Bill, allowed the Supreme Court to hear only the cases that the Court thought were most important. The goal was to reduce the backlog of cases that made it to the Supreme Court and help streamline the judicial system. Taft had wanted to reform the court system for many years. His first published legal papers, way back in 1884, had dealt with that very subject. He had tried to make changes in the system while he was president, but he had not received cooperation and nothing got done.

Taft served as chief justice under three presidents: Warren G. Harding, Calvin Coolidge, and Herbert Hoover. The other members of the Supreme Court called Taft "Big Chief," a name he loved.

OPINIONS AND DECISIONS

In Taft's view, important matters like guilt and innocence and right and wrong should be decided by people with the proper training—judges. For this reason, he was opposed to the

While Taft held the position of chief justice, three different presidents held office, including Calvin Coolidge (left) and Herbert Hoover (right).

——————————————— ✧ ———————————————

jury trial, at which a jury of peers decides whether a person accused of a crime is guilty or innocent. Taft thought that juries were more likely than judges to reach bad decisions.

It is a common legal saying—dating back to at least the 1700s—that it is better for ninety-nine guilty persons to go free than for one innocent person to go to jail. In a jury trial, an accused person must be found guilty "beyond a reasonable doubt" to be convicted of a crime. But Taft felt that juries that were easily fooled were ruining the justice system by sending guilty criminals back onto the streets too often. As far as he was concerned, too much attention was being paid to protecting criminals' rights.

Taft also believed that the rules of justice were too complex. Too many court cases were being thrown out because of technicalities—because the rules had not been properly followed. He wanted to simplify these rules. His positions on the criminal justice system did not take hold, however. The rules of justice have grown more complicated over the years, there are more jury trials than ever, and the rights of defendants are still protected.

As chief justice, Taft was best known for his reforms of the federal court system and for his key role in getting a separate new building for the Supreme Court, which had offices in several buildings over the years. Taft believed that the judicial branch of government deserved a permanent home, just as the executive and legislative branches had their own buildings— the White House and the Capitol Building. (While Taft was chief justice, the Supreme Court met in the Capitol Building.)

Taft's Supreme Court decisions also upheld the income tax amendment and the so-called Prohibition laws. These laws had been in effect since 1919. Taft saw to it that bootleggers, those who made money from illegally selling liquor, were convicted and put in jail.

THE TEMPERANCE CRUSADE.
FOUR HOURS IN A BAR ROOM.

1ST HOUR
CYNICAL INDIFFERENCE.

2ND HOUR
MOCKERY AND DEFIANCE.

3RD HOUR
RAGE AND DESPAIR.

4TH HOUR
UNCONDITIONAL SURRENDER.

———————— ✧

This 1874 cartoon from the temperance movement (a movement to moderate or abstain from drinking liquor) describes a bartender's reaction to Prohibition.

Taft and Nellie strongly disagreed about Prohibition, one of the most controversial social issues of the day. Having stopped drinking, Taft came to believe that alcohol was evil and should be banned. Nellie believed that the laws could not be enforced and were, in essence, creating criminals. History favored Nellie's position. Alcoholic beverages have been legal in the United States since 1933, when Prohibition ended.

FAILING HEALTH

Taft's health had begun to decline in 1924. He had two heart attacks that year, the first in February and the second at the end of April.

Even as he was getting weaker, Taft continued to live in Washington and serve on the Supreme Court. He had an electric elevator installed in his house so he could get up to his third-floor office without having to take the stairs.

Taft's brother Charles died in Cincinnati in December 1929. Taft's doctors warned him that he was not strong enough to travel to Ohio to attend the funeral, but he went anyway. When he returned to Washington, he was so weak that he had to be hospitalized.

A LAUGH SILENCED

Friends and relatives were quite concerned about Taft, who was seventy-two years old. His laugh, once so loud and hearty, had grown weak. After his hospitalization, he never returned to an active life. He last sat with the Supreme Court on January 6, 1930. On February 3, he announced his retirement. He had been in public service for almost fifty years.

Taft's grave (right) *lies in Arlington National Cemetery, along with the graves of other chief justices and national heroes.*

——————————— ✧

By the beginning of March, Taft's heart was so bad that he was slipping in and out of a coma. He died quietly on March 8, 1930.

Taft's funeral was the first funeral ever broadcast live on radio, and he became the first U.S. president to be buried in Arlington National Cemetery outside of Washington, D.C. (Although all U.S. presidents are eligible to be buried in Arlington, only Taft and John F. Kennedy are buried there. Most presidents choose to be buried in a family plot or on grounds with more personal sentimental value.) Nellie outlived her husband by thirteen years. She died on May 22, 1943, and was buried beside her husband.

TIMELINE

1857 William Howard Taft is born on September 15 in Cincinnati, Ohio, the son of Alphonso Taft, a distinguished judge, and Louise Taft.

1874 Taft graduates from Woodward High School in Cincinnati.

1878 Taft graduates from Yale University.

1879 Taft meets Helen "Nellie" Herron.

1880 After graduating from Cincinnati Law School, Taft passes the bar exam and receives his license to practice law. Working as assistant prosecuting attorney for Hamilton County, Ohio, Taft serves in public office for the first time.

1882 Taft briefly serves as tax collector for the Cincinnati area.

1883 Taft establishes a private law practice.

1885 Taft is appointed assistant county solicitor for Hamilton County. In May, after several marriage proposals from Taft, Nellie finally accepts.

1886 Taft and Nellie Herron are married on June 19.

1887 Taft is appointed judge in the Cincinnati Superior Court and serves until 1890.

1889 Robert Alphonso Taft, the Tafts' first child, is born on September 8.

1890 Taft begins his appointment as U.S. solicitor general, a position he holds for two years.

1891 Alphonso Taft, William's father, dies in San Diego, California. The Tafts' second child, Helen Herron Taft, is born on August 1.

1892	President Benjamin Harrison appoints Taft judge in the U.S. Sixth Circuit Court of Appeals.
1897	The Tafts' third child, Charles Phelps Taft, is born on September 20.
1901	Taft is officially appointed the first civilian governor of the Philippines by President McKinley.
1903	President Theodore Roosevelt names Taft to a cabinet position, secretary of war.
1904–1908	Taft oversees the construction of the Panama Canal.
1905	Taft travels to Japan for a meeting with Japanese premier Count Katsura to help smooth relations between Japan and the United States and to negotiate a peace treaty between Japan and Russia.
1906	Taft helps negotiate peace with rebels in Cuba.
1908	Taft wins the Republican Party's presidential nomination. In November Taft is elected president of the United States, defeating Democratic candidate William Jennings Bryan.
1909	Taft is inaugurated as the twenty-seventh president of the United States. Responding to demands for lower tariffs, Taft accepts a compromise tariff bill, the Payne-Aldrich Tariff Act.
1912	Taft is nominated for reelection by the Republicans. Theodore Roosevelt leaves the Republican Party and runs for another term as president on the Progressive Party or "Bull Moose" ticket. In the presidential election, Roosevelt and Taft split the Republican vote, allowing the Democratic candidate, Woodrow Wilson, to win the presidency.
1913	Taft becomes a law professor at Yale University.

1918 Taft becomes joint chairperson of the National War Labor Board.

1921 Fulfilling his lifelong ambition, Taft is appointed chief justice of the U.S. Supreme Court by President Warren G. Harding.

1924 Taft suffers two heart attacks, one in February and one in April.

1929 Taft's brother Charles dies in Cincinnati. Taft is warned by his doctors not to travel to the funeral, but he goes anyway. He is soon hospitalized for his failing health.

1930 In February Taft announces his retirement from the Supreme Court. He dies on March 8 in Washington, D.C. He is buried in Arlington National Cemetery.

SOURCE NOTES

7 "President William Taft Baseball Attendance," *Baseball Almanac*, 2000, <http://www.baseball-almanac.com/prz_qwt.shtml> (January 21, 2004).

9 Henry F. Pringle, *William Howard Taft: The Life and Times,* vol. 1 (Newtown, CT: American Political Biography Press, 1939), 22.

9 Ibid., 3.

17 Ibid., 31.

17 Ibid., 35.

23 Ibid., 60.

24 Judith Icke Anderson, *William Howard Taft: An Intimate Portrait* (New York: W. W. Norton & Co., 1981), 46.

31 Ibid., 50.

33 Pringle, 78.

33 Ibid., 81.

36 Anderson, 60.

40 Alpheus Thomas Mason, *William Howard Taft: Chief Justice* (New York: Simon & Schuster, 1965), 18.

43 Anderson, 22.

47 Ibid., 70.

56 Mrs. W. H. Taft, *Recollections of Full Years* (New York: Dodd, Mead, & Co., 1914), 35.

57 Ibid.

57 Anderson, 84.

58 Melissa Maupin, *William Howard Taft: Our Twenty-seventh President* (Chanhassen, MN: The Child's World, 2002), 21.

63 Mason, 30.

63 Anderson, 92.

64 Ibid., 98.

65 Ibid., 109.

66 Ibid., 112.

69 Ibid., 231.

69 Maupin, 23.

71 Ibid., 124.

75 Ibid., 15.

77 Pringle, 459.

82 Ibid., 515.

88 Maupin, 32.

90 Anderson, 27.

92 John A. Gable, "Roosevelt, Theodore," *World Book Online Reference Centre*, n.d., <http://www.worldbookonline.com/ar?/na/ar/co/ar474860.htm> (October 7, 2003).

92 Anderson, 14.

95 Ibid., 259.

95 Ibid., 255.

98 Mason, 57.

Selected Bibliography

Anderson, Judith Icke. *William Howard Taft: An Intimate Portrait.* New York: W. W. Norton & Co., 1981.

Casey, Jane Clark. *William Howard Taft.* Danbury, CT: Children's Press, 1989.

Dickson, Paul. *The New Dickson Baseball Dictionary.* New York: Harvest Books, 1999.

Joseph, Paul. *William Taft.* Edina, MN: Abdo, 2001.

Mason, Alpheus Thomas. *William Howard Taft: Chief Justice.* New York: Simon & Schuster, 1965.

Maupin, Melissa. *William Howard Taft: Our Twenty-seventh President.* Chanhassen, MN: The Child's World, 2002.

Pringle, Henry F. *William Howard Taft: The Life and Times.* Vol. 1. Newtown, CT: American Political Biography Press, 1939.

Schlossberg, Dan. *The New Baseball Catalog.* New York: Jonathan David, 1998.

Taft, Mrs. W. H. *Recollections of Full Years.* New York: Dodd, Mead, & Co., 1914.

Further Reading and Websites

Davis, Kenneth C. *Don't Know Much about the Presidents.* New York: HarperCollins Juvenile Books, 2001.

DeGregorio, William A., and Connie Jo Dickerson. *The Complete Book of U.S. Presidents.* New York: Random House, 1997.

DuTemple, Lesley A. *The Panama Canal.* Minneapolis: Lerner Publications Company, 2003.

Kowalski, Kathiann M. *Order in the Court: A Look at the Judicial Branch.* Minneapolis: Lerner Publications Company, 2004.

Landau, Elaine. *Warren G. Harding*. Minneapolis: Lerner Publications Company, 2005.

MacPherson, Stephanie Sammartino. *Theodore Roosevelt*. Minneapolis: Lerner Publications Company, 2005.

Sauer, Patrick. *The Complete Idiot's Guide to American Presidents*. Indianapolis, IN: Alpha Books, 2000.

"William Howard Taft." *The American Presidency.* <http://www.americanpresident.org> This site about the history and functions of the presidency includes a biography of "the Reluctant President."

"William Howard Taft." *Arlington National Cemetery.* <http://www.arlingtoncemetery.com/whtaft.htm> The Arlington National Cemetery site contains information about Taft's burial site. He was the first U.S. president to be buried in this national cemetery.

"William Howard Taft." *The White House.* <http://www.whitehouse.gov/history/presidents/wt27.html> The official White House site contains biographies of all the presidents and first ladies.

"William Howard Taft Biography." *Grolier/The American Presidency.* <http://www.gi.grolier.com/presidents/ea/bios/27ptaft.html> *Grolier Multimedia Encyclopedia* offers detailed presidential biographies and bibliographies.

"William Howard Taft Inaugural Address." *Bartleby.com.* <http://www.bartleby.com/124/pres43.html> This site includes the complete text of Taft's inaugural speech, given on March 4, 1909.

"William Howard Taft National Historic Site." *National Park Service.* <http://www.nps.gov/who> This is the National Park Service site about the house in Cincinnati, Ohio, where William Howard Taft was born.

INDEX

ABOUT THE AUTHOR

Michael Benson was born in Rochester, New York, and graduated from Hofstra University with a major in communication arts. In 1987 he married Lisa Grasso, an attorney. They have two children, Tekla and Matthew. The family lives in Brooklyn, New York. Benson is the former editor of *The Military Technical Journal* and the author of more than thirty books, including biographies of Bill Clinton, Gloria Estefan, and Malcolm X.

PHOTO ACKNOWLEDGMENTS

The images in this book are used with the permission of: The White House, pp. 1, 7, 9, 17, 31, 36, 47, 58, 69, 82, 95; Cincinnati Historical Society, pp. 2, 15, 16, 32, 39, 43, 91, 93; Library of Congress, pp. 6 [LC-USZ62-122312], 10 [LC-USZ62-095931], 19 [LC-D4-39341], 20 [LC-D4-39330], 24 [LC-USZ61-1156], 30 [LC-USZ62-25804], 37 [LC-USZ62-096500], 44 [LC-USZ62-115917], 45 [LC-USZ62-075755], 46 [LC-USZ62-117979], 49 [LC-USZ62-132301], 52, [LC-USZ62-103380], 53 [LC-USZC2-6274], 54 [LC-USZ62-124242], 59 [LC-USZ62-083103], 64 [LC-USZ62-095705], 67 [LC-USZ62-108094], 68 [LC-USZ62-228], 70 [LC-USZ62-132298], 72 [LC-USZ62-41721], 73 [LC-USZ62-111462], 78 [LC-USZ62-091029], 80 [LC-D418-73523], 81 [LC-USZ62-094731], 83 (left) [LC-USZ62-103915], 83 (right) [LC-USZ62-076997], 86 [LC-USZ62-095932], 89 [LC-USZ62-088502], 94 [LC-H824-T-2397-001-B], 96 [LC-USZ62-90044], 98 [LC-USZ62-91485], 100 (left); Ohio Historical Society, p. 11; Taft National Historical Park, pp. 12, 14; From the Collection of the Public Library of Cincinnati and Hamilton County, pp. 21, 26; Hulton|Archive by Getty Images, p. 34; © Bettmann/CORBIS, pp. 50, 61, 74; Courtesy Ohio State University Cartoon Research Library, p. 76; Courtesy Louis D. Brandeis School of Law Library, p. 84; © David J. and Janice L. Frent Collection/CORBIS, p. 88; National Archives, p. 100 (right); © CORBIS, p. 101; Courtesy Arlington National Cemetery, p.103.

Front cover: Library of Congress [LC-USZ62-13027].